TWO DOZEN
DINOSAURS

A FIRST BOOK OF DINOSAUR FACTS, MYSTERIES, GAMES AND FUN

Catherine Ripley

Illustrations by Bo-Kim Louie

Owl

GREEY DE PENCIER BOOKS

To *Chickadee* readers everywhere who asked such wonderful questions about dinosaurs. Keep on asking!

Consultant: Kevin Seymour, Department of Vertebrate Paleontology, Royal Ontario Museum

Special thanks to my editor Sheba Meland,
to designer Cliff Smith and to Bo-Kim Louie for her magical illustrations.

Catherine Ripley

Books from OWL are published by Greey de Pencier Books,
179 John Street, Suite 500 Toronto, Ontario M5T 3G5

The Owl colophon is a trademark of the Young Naturalist Foundation.
Greey de Pencier Books is a licensed user of the trademarks of the Young Naturalist Foundation.

This book was published with the generous support of the Canada Council and the Ontario Arts Council.

Canadian Cataloguing in Publication Data

Ripley, Catherine, 1957 —
Two dozen dinosaurs
ISBN 0-920775-55-1

1. Dinosaurs — Juvenile literature. 2. Puzzles —
Juvenile literature. 3. Games — Juvenile literature.

I. Louie, Bo-Kim, 1954 —   . II. Title
QE862.D5R56 1991   j567.9'1   C90-095271

Cover art: Leo Monahan
Design: Wycliffe Smith
Printed in Hong Kong

C   D   E   F

INTRODUCTION

Imagine: dinosaurs lived millions of years ago, before any man or woman or child ever lived on Earth. The only way we know anything about them is from their fossils — ancient bones, skin imprints, footprints and eggs that have been buried under layers and layers of earth for millions of years. ◆ ◆ ◆ ◆ Scientists dig up these rock-hard fossils and from them make some good guesses about what dinosaur days were like. But new fossils are being discovered all the time, and these discoveries change the scientists' guesses. ◆ ◆ ◆ ◆ So then, what do scientists know for *sure* about every single dinosaur that ever lived? They know that all dinosaurs were land animals that lived 65 to 230 million years ago. They know that all dinosaurs walked with their legs right under their bodies just as you do and your cat does and a bird does. They know that all dinosaurs had one of two types of hip bones: they were either "bird-hipped" or "lizard-hipped." And that's it. Amazingly, scientists know just these three facts that apply to all dinosaurs. ◆ ◆ ◆ ◆ Of course, scientists know much more about individual dinosaurs. You'll find many of their discoveries in this book, so dig in and let the dinosaurs dazzle you! ◆ ◆ ◆ ◆

MEET TWO DOZEN
DINOSAURS

■ Here are a few of the many, many dinosaurs that have been discovered so far. (You'll meet all of them again in this book.) Like all dinosaurs, they can be divided into two groups by looking at their hip bones. ◆ Scientists group dinosaurs in this way because it is their hip bones that made dinosaurs different from the sprawling, crawling land creatures that came before them.

The ornithiscians, the "bird-hipped" dinosaurs, have hip bones that look like this.

The saurischians, the "lizard-hipped" dinosaurs, have hip bones that look like this.

Can you spot 9 ornithiscians and 15 saurischians in this line-up?

COELOPHYSIS
see-lo-*fye*-sis

DEINONYCHOSAUR
dine-*on*-ih-ko-sore

IGUANODON
ig-*wan*-oh-don

ORNITHOMIMUS
or-nith-o-*mime*-us

BRACHIOSAURUS
brak-ee-uh-sore-us

PROTOCERATOPS
pro-toe-*sair*-ah-tops

DROMICEIOMIMUS
dro-mi-see-o-*mime*-us

BARYONYX
bar-ee-*on*-ix

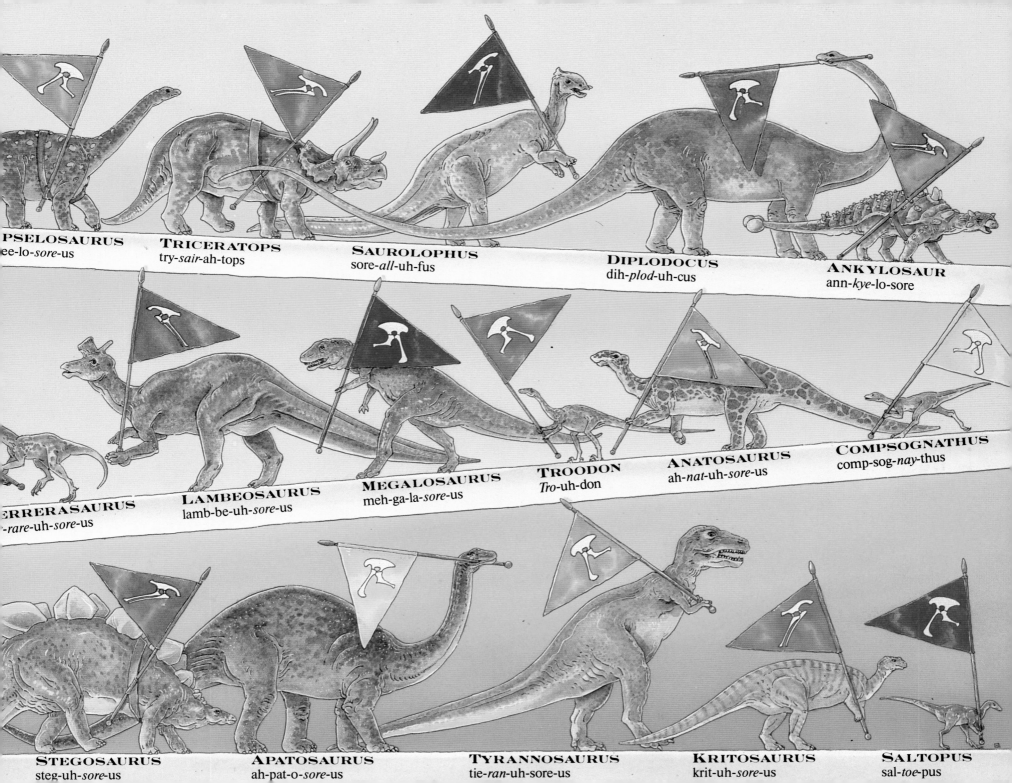

PSELOSAURUS
ee-lo-*sore*-us

TRICERATOPS
try-*sair*-ah-tops

SAUROLOPHUS
sore-*all*-uh-fus

DIPLODOCUS
dih-*plod*-uh-cus

ANKYLOSAUR
ann-*kye*-lo-sore

ERRERASAURUS
-rare-uh-*sore*-us

LAMBEOSAURUS
lamb-be-uh-*sore*-us

MEGALOSAURUS
meh-ga-la-*sore*-us

TROODON
Tro-uh-don

ANATOSAURUS
ah-*nat*-uh-*sore*-us

COMPSOGNATHUS
comp-sog-*nay*-thus

STEGOSAURUS
steg-uh-*sore*-us

APATOSAURUS
ah-pat-o-*sore*-us

TYRANNOSAURUS
tie-*ran*-uh-sore-us

KRITOSAURUS
krit-uh-*sore*-us

SALTOPUS
sal-*toe*-pus

HOW BIG
WERE THEY?

Some dinosaurs were *huge*. Others were tiny. ◆ To find out how big some dinosaurs were, follow the maze path.

At each stop, read the question and then choose an answer. ◆ If you're right, the path will lead you to the next dinosaur. If you're wrong, try again!

START

FINISH

Yes, it was bigger. It was as big as a rooster.

YES

Was **COMPSOGNATHUS** bigger than a robin?

NO

YES

Was **BRACHIOSAURUS** bigger than a blue whale?

NO

No. Amazingly, a blue whale is as long as 2 school buses and weighs as much as 25 elephants. **BRACHIOSAURUS** was as long as 1¾ school buses and weighed as much as 13 elephants.

Yes, it was a bit taller and weighed whole lot more — as much as an elephant!

6

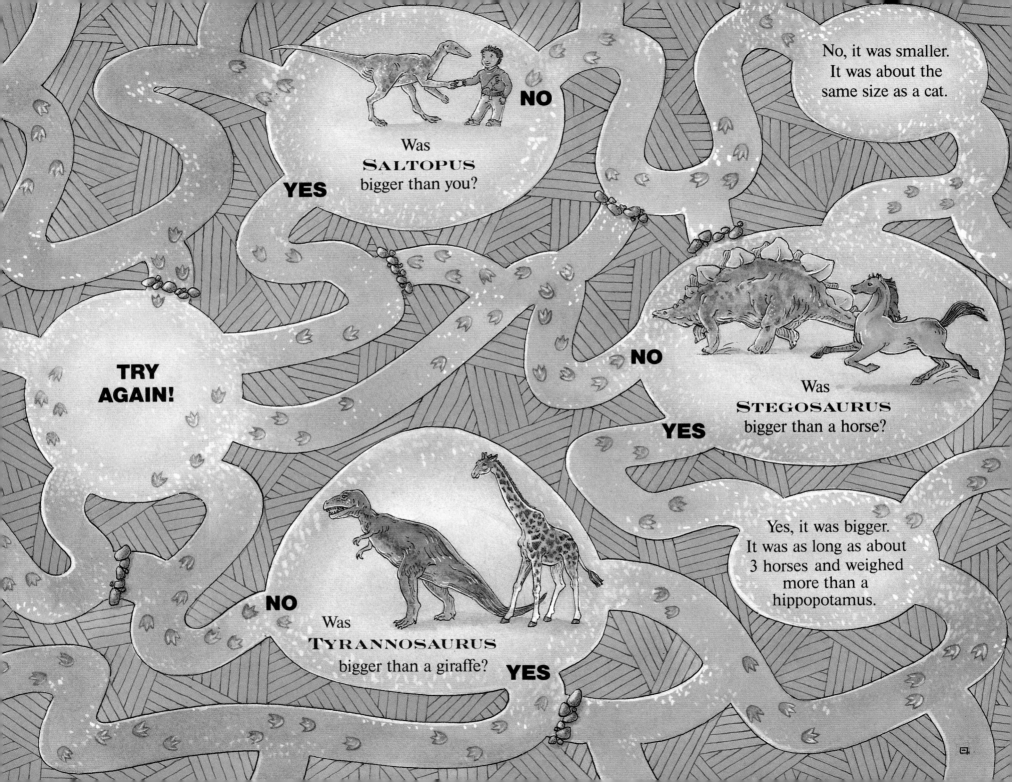

IF DINOSAURS COULD BRAG

■ If dinosaurs could brag, what would they brag about? ◆ Here are some guesses based on what scientists have found so far. ◆ Can you match up each bragger with its name and description?

TYRANNOSAURUS REX, the largest meat-eating dinosaur yet discovered, was probably the fiercest dinosaur of all.

TROODON, also a meat-eater, had a relatively larger brain than other dinosaurs. A bigger brain often means a smarter animal.

HERRERASAURUS is the oldest dinosaur found so far. Discovered in Argentina, the skeleton dates back about 230 million years.

I'm the fiercest!

I lay the biggest eggs!

No other known dinosaur could catch up to **DROMICEIOMIMUS** running at full speed. This small meat-eating dinosaur probably ran a little faster than an Olympic runner.

DIPLODOCUS, a huge plant-eating dinosaur, was as long as two school buses parked in a line, but weighed much, much less.

SAUROLOPHUS, a plant-eating dinosaur, was one of the many types of dinosaurs in the "duckbill" family that thrived at the end of dinosaur days. Duckbills also had more teeth in their mouths than any other dinosaur. When old ones fell out, new ones grew in. A duckbill could have 2000 teeth in one lifetime!

HYPSELOSAURUS, another large plant-eater, laid the biggest eggs found so far. Each of its eggs was as long as five big chicken eggs end to end and was four eggs wide.

I'm the fastest!

AN EGG-CITING
DISCOVERY

■ In 1922, scientists dug up some nest mounds full of potato-sized fossil eggs in Mongolia. No one had ever seen eggs like these before. Could dinosaurs have laid them? ◆ When they discovered some adult and baby PROTOCERATOPS skeletons nearby, the scientists knew they could answer *yes*!

Here is a PROTOCERATOPS family scene from 65 million years ago. ◆ How many eggs can you count? How many newly- hatched babies are there? How many older babies? How many adults? How many altogether?

Answers on page 32.

LUNCH
PLEASE!

Imagine if some dinosaurs arrived for lunch in this fast-food restaurant. What would they order? ◆ **Use the clues about their teeth to choose the best meal from the menu for each dinosaur here.**

MEGALOSAURUS had razor-sharp teeth for biting into skin and flesh.

APATOSAURUS had peg-like teeth for tearing off leaves that it then gulped down whole. It also swallowed stones to help grind up the leaves in its stomach.

LAMBEOSAURUS had row upon row of blunt teeth for munching vegetation for lunch. When the teeth wore out, new ones grew in to fill their places.

BARYONYX had teeth and a snout much like that of a crocodile. It probably ate fish.

Answers on page 32.

Soft Drinks	.75
Green Salad	1.49
Carrot Sticks	.85
Orange	.75
Apple	.85
Banana	

TYRANNOSAURUS TALE

One morning, just as the ☼ rose above the trees, a young **TYRANNOSAURUS REX** set out to hunt. She was tired of chasing 🦟 and 🦎 and opossums.

She had to work so hard and catch so many to fill her up that she always seemed to be hungry.

Today she would go after something bigger!

Just over the hill, 🦖 saw a single **ANKYLOSAUR** munching on some . Down the hill she charged, but the great big 🐢 heard her.

It turned and started lashing its tail back and forth. **Bang!** The hard tail knocked 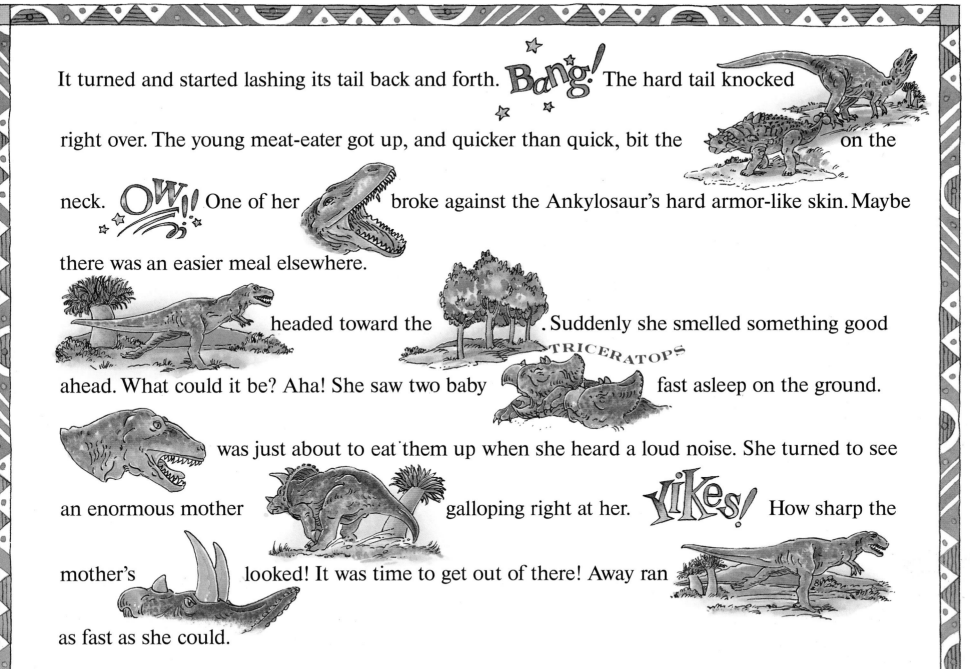 right over. The young meat-eater got up, and quicker than quick, bit the on the neck. **OW!!** One of her broke against the Ankylosaur's hard armor-like skin. Maybe there was an easier meal elsewhere. headed toward the . Suddenly she smelled something good ahead. What could it be? Aha! She saw two baby fast asleep on the ground. was just about to eat them up when she heard a loud noise. She turned to see an enormous mother galloping right at her. **Yikes!** How sharp the mother's looked! It was time to get out of there! Away ran as fast as she could.

When  stopped running, she found herself near a marsh. Ahead she saw a group of twenty IGUANODONS chewing on ferns. Maybe she could catch one of the five . As she moved closer, the biggest saw her coming.

Suddenly the adults made a big circle around their babies. They shook their spiky at . She knew she was outnumbered.

Where could find food? Ahead she saw a tiny, slender ORNITHOMIMUS

chasing after a . Surely she could catch this little creature. But when the heard the big dinosaur ZOOM — it was gone just like a bolt of .

stopped. She sniffed the air. She could smell fresh meat nearby.

She crept over the next and saw three DEINONYCHOSAURS feasting on a duckbill dinosaur they'd hunted down. This was it! The hungry young meat-eater let out a mighty *Roar*

and then charged down the hill. The three  were so startled they ran away,

leaving their dinner behind. ate and ate and ate — until she was full to

bursting. *BURP!* Now it was time for a long nap in the setting

DINOSAURS
OR NOT?

All of these creatures lived in dinosaur days, but most of them aren't even dinosaurs!

To figure out who's who, pick out the pairs. ◆ The animals by themselves are dinosaurs. The ones with mates are not.

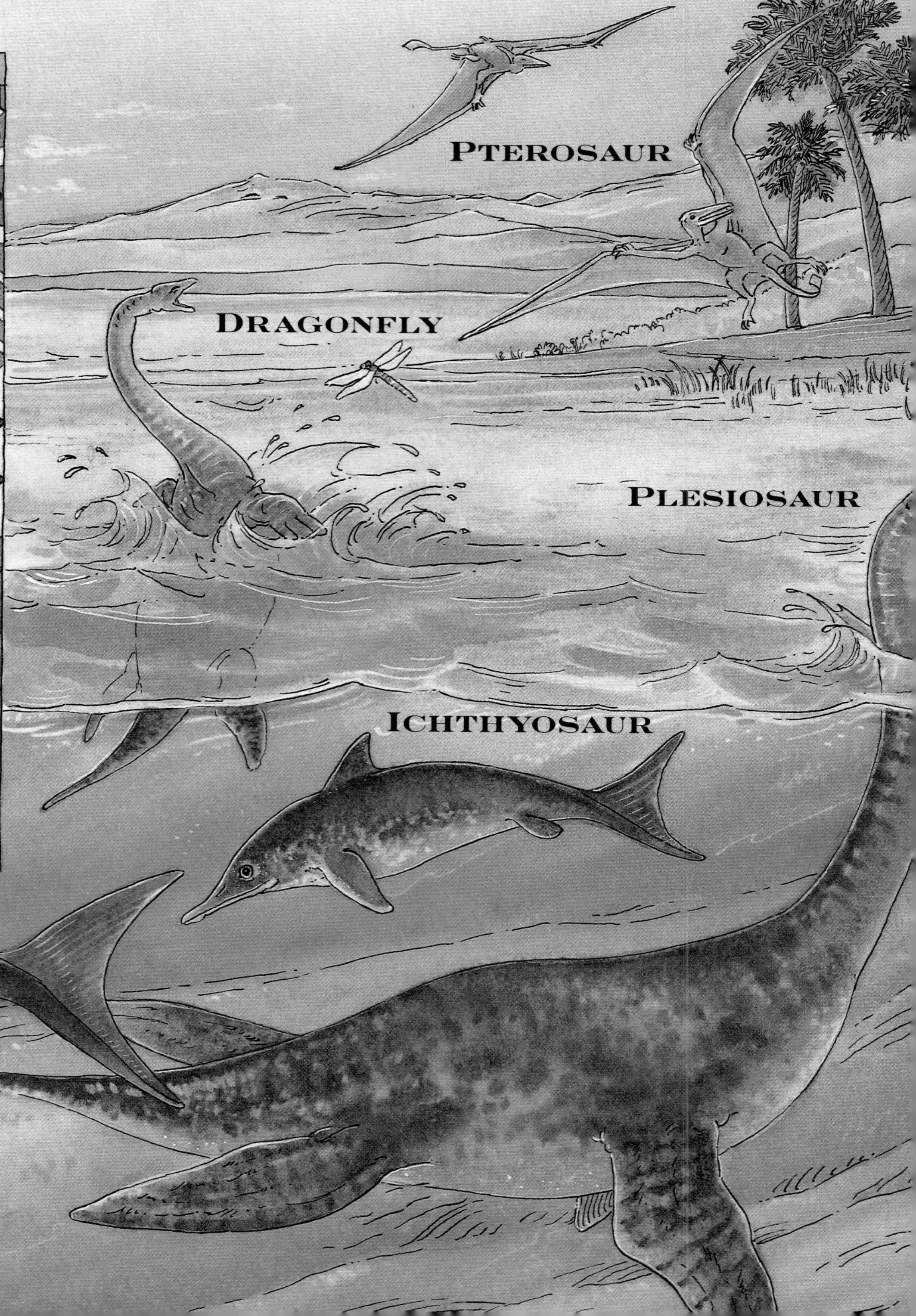

PTEROSAUR

DRAGONFLY

PLESIOSAUR

ICHTHYOSAUR

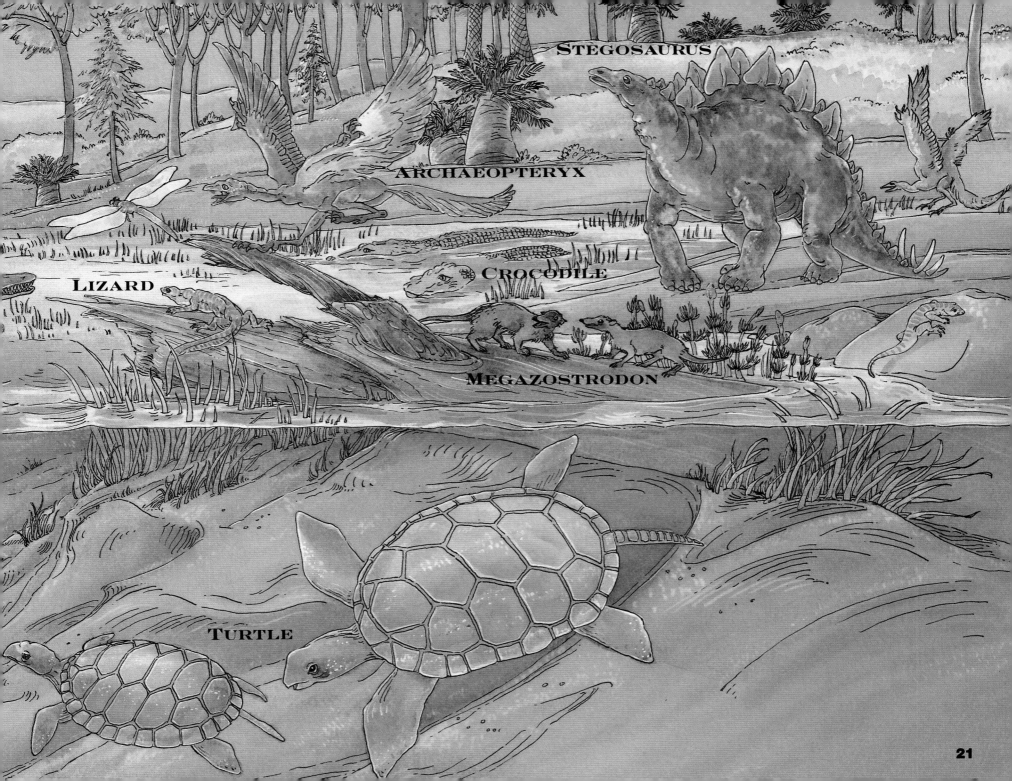

STEGOSAURUS

ARCHAEOPTERYX

LIZARD

CROCODILE

MEGAZOSTRODON

TURTLE

TRAVEL
BACK IN TIME

■ **WHOOSH. Away you go —** back, back, back 200 million years to a spot somewhere in what is now New Mexico.

You are back in what paleontologists call the Triassic period. ◆ There's one of the earliest dinosaurs, Coelophysis.

Phew! It's warm.

Triassic period ◆ **The beginning of the dinosaur age**

AND TRAVEL AGAIN

■ **WHOOSH. Away you go again.** This time you travel forward 135 million years to the very same spot. ◆ Now it's the end of the Cretaceous period. ◆ Where's that cool salty breeze coming from?

What other differences can you spot here?

Answer on page 32.

FOSSIL
FIND

 Finding a fossil — any trace of a plant or animal that lived from thousands to millions of years ago — is rare. ◆ That's because the conditions for making fossils have to be just right.

Sand or silt has to fill in quickly over the animal or plant remains so that the sun and wind and rain don't destroy them. ◆ Only then do these traces turn hard as rock as they are "fossilized" and preserved for people to find millions of years later.

Here's a scientist working on a museum exhibit about fossils. But something's wacky! Which of these things really are ancient fossils? Which are not?

Answers on page 32.

DINOSAUR
MYSTERIES

■ Fossils can only tell scientists so much about an ancient animal, and the discovery of a whole fossil skeleton is rare. ◆ Dinosaur scientists, called paleontologists, make many good guesses about dinosaurs, but there are still a number of puzzling mysteries they haven't solved. Are you a good detective? ◆ Perhaps one day *you'll* solve some of these mysteries!

Did all dinosaurs lay eggs?

Maybe not. Some scientists think that several dinosaurs, such as **COELOPHYSIS** and **APATASAURUS**, may have had live babies.

Was **TYRANNOSAURUS** really the fiercest?

Maybe not. Although smaller, **DEINONYCHOSAUR** was probably quicker and more agile than **TYRANNOSAURUS**. It also may have hunted in packs. Which one would you want to face?

What color were the dinosaurs?

Were some dinosaurs bright red, blue and yellow like a parrot or vibrant green like a frog? Did any have stripes or spots, like zebras and leopards, to help them hide? No one knows for sure.

Why did many dinosaurs grow so-o-o-o big?

No one knows. It could be that their jumbo size was a good defense against meat-eating dinosaurs, or that the huge beasts could stay warm longer in cool weather.

Did any dinosaurs swim?

Scientists used to think that **BRACHIOSAURUS** spent all its time in water. Most now agree that this huge dinosaur lived mainly on land, perhaps plunging into water to get rid of lice or bugs. Duckbills may have dived into the water to escape their meat-eating enemies, but more likely relied on their keen senses to detect danger before it came too near.

Is **BRACHIOSAURUS** the biggest dinosaur?

Probably not. Recently three new dinosaur skeletons have been discovered. "Supersaurus," "Ultrasaurus" and "Seismosaurus" may be even bigger, towering over the four-storey high Brachiosaurus by a storey or more respectively. Scientists, however, haven't yet finished working with the skeletons.

Are birds living dinosaurs?

It's very likely. Most scientists believe that **ARCHAEOPTERYX**, the oldest known bird, could be related to a group of small meat-eating dinosaurs called **COELOSAURS**. Of course, **ARCHAEOPTERYX** had feathers and the **COELOSAURS** didn't.
But except for the wishbone, the skeletons of these two creatures *are* similar. So the next time you see a bird on the wing, you might be watching a dinosaur fly by!

What did STEGOSAURUS use its back plates for?

Some think the plates were used for protection. Others wonder if they were used as solar panels that trapped the sun's heat to help **STEGOSAURUS** keep warm.

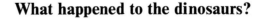

What happened to the dinosaurs?

Did the climate get too cold or too hot for the dinosaurs? Did an asteroid from outer space smash into the earth, sending up big clouds of dust and dirt, which blocked out the sun and killed the plants most dinosaurs ate? No one knows for sure. But scientists do know that something *big* happened 65 million years ago to bring an end to dinosaur days.

MAKE YOUR OWN
DINOSAURS

■ You won't see a STEGOSAURUS out your window today, but imagine what life would be like if dinosaurs were still around! ◆ Mix up a batch of play clay and make your very own dinosaur world.

Play Clay Recipe Ask an adult to help.

- 500 mL (2 cups) flour
- 500 mL (2 cups) water
- 30 mL (2 tbsp.) cream of tartar
- 250 mL (1 cup) salt
- 30 mL (2 tbsp.) oil
- food coloring (several colors)

1. In a bowl, mix all the ingredients except the food coloring.
2. Decide how many colors of clay you want. Pour enough of the mixture for one color into a pot.
3. Add a few drops of food coloring and stir over low heat until the mixture forms a ball and is cooked through. Remove and let cool.
4. After washing the pot, repeat steps 2 and 3 for each of the other colors.

FOSSIL
DETECTIVE

■ **Sometimes paleontologists find fossil footprints imprinted in a rock, which show that an ancient creature once walked there.** ◆ **Other times they find the ghostly shapes of leaves, flowers and shells from dinosaur days.**

Once the finding is over, the puzzling begins! ◆ **Which dinosaur made the footprints? Which creature lived in that shell?**

Make some of your own imprints and get your friends and family puzzling! Here's how:

Flatten out a fistful of play clay on a table top. Collect some small things such as an elastic band, bottle cap, leftover bone, paper clip, crayon, leaf and so on. Carefully press each object into the play clay and then remove and hide the objects. Who can identify which things made the imprints?

ANSWERS

An Egg-citing Discovery page 12

There are 50 eggs, 3 newly hatched babies, 2 older babies and 2 adults. Altogether there are 57 **PROTOCERATOPS**.

Lunch, Please! page 14

LAMBEOSAURUS would order any of the fruit or vegetable dishes. **APATASAURUS** would order the same plus a serving of stone soup. **MEGALOSAURUS** would order any of the meat dishes. **BARYONYX** would probably order the fish dish.

Travel Back in Time page 22

Look at the dinosaur, the background, the magnolia flowers and the **PTEROSAUR**. **COELOPHYSIS**, the dinosaur in the first picture, lived only at the beginning of dinosaur days. At that time New Mexico was mostly dry desert. Gingko trees were just starting to grow.

By the time of the second picture, 135 million years later, a giant inland sea had formed near New Mexico. For the first time, flowering plants covered the earth. **KRITOSAURUS** was one of the many duckbills that only lived on the earth near the end of dinosaur days. The **PTEROSAUR** is still in the picture, but note how much bigger it is than its relative 135 million years earlier.

Fossil Find page 24

The wacky things are the skipping rope, baseball cap, skateboard and bottle. The fossils are the footprints, the dinosaur skeleton, the trilobite skeleton, the stone eggs, the bones and the leaf imprint, but of course, it is unlikely that all of these fossils would be found together naturally like this anywhere in the world!